Fighting Fire
Fire Stations in Action

by Mari Schuh

Consulting Editor: Gail Saunders-Smith, PhD

Consultant: Keith S. Frangiamore, Vice President of Operations
Fire Safety Consultants Inc., Elgin, Illinois

Capstone
press

Mankato, Minnesota

Pebble Plus is published by Capstone Press,
151 Good Counsel Drive, P.O. Box 669, Mankato, Minnesota 56002.
www.capstonepress.com

1 2 3 4 5 6 14 13 12 11 10 09

Library of Congress Cataloging-in-Publication Data
Schuh, Mari C., 1975–
    Fire stations in action / by Mari Schuh.
    p. cm. — (Pebble plus. Fighting fire)
    Includes bibliographical references and index.
    Summary: "In simple text and photos, presents fire stations and what firefighters do" — Provided by publisher.
    ISBN-13: 978-1-4296-1724-6 (hardcover)
    ISBN-10: 1-4296-1724-1 (hardcover)
    1. Fire stations — Juvenile literature. I. Title. II. Series
TH9148.S38 2009
628.9'25 — dc22
                                                    2008026955

Editorial Credits
Sarah L. Schuette, editor; Tracy Davies, designer; Marcy Morin, photo shoot scheduler

Photo Credits
Capstone Press/Karon Dubke, all

The author dedicates this book to the Gaul family of Sergeant Bluff, Iowa.

Note to Parents and Teachers

The Fighting Fire set supports national science standards related to science, technology, and
society. This book describes and illustrates fire stations in action. The images support early
readers in understanding the text. The repetition of words and phrases helps early readers
learn new words. This book also introduces early readers to subject-specific vocabulary words,
which are defined in the Glossary section. Early readers may need assistance to read some
words and to use the Table of Contents, Glossary, Read More, Internet Sites, and Index
sections of the book.

Table of Contents

Busy Fire Stations

Fire stations are always
ready for emergencies.
Fire stations have fire trucks
and lots of gear inside.

Firefighters work
at fire stations
day and night.
They are always busy.

At the Station

Firefighters clean fire trucks and fire stations often.

Firefighters make sure
their gear works well.
They train to learn
new skills.

Firefighters exercise
at the fire station.
They need to be strong
to carry people
out of burning buildings.

Firefighters cook
and eat meals together
like a family.
Some firefighters even sleep
at the fire station.

To the Rescue

A loud alarm sounds

at the fire station.

It's time to put out a fire.

Firefighters quickly put on
their bunker gear.
They jump on a fire truck
and race to the scene.

A Good Team

Firefighters work as a team

to put out the fire.

Then, they go back

to the fire station.

Good job, team!

Glossary

alarm — a buzzer or bell that gives a warning; dispatchers sound an alarm to tell firefighters there is a fire.

bunker gear — the heavy coat, pants, and boots firefighters wear to protect themselves from being burned

exercise — physical activity people do to stay fit and healthy; firefighters often exercise at the fire station to stay strong.

gear — clothing and equipment; firefighter gear includes coats, pants, boots, helmets, face masks, hoses, and axes.

Read More

Anderson, Sheila. *Fire Station.* First Step Nonfiction. Community Buildings. Minneapolis: Lerner Classroom, 2008.

Gordon, Sharon. *What's Inside a Firehouse?* Bookworms. What's Inside? New York: Benchmark Books, 2007.

Internet Sites

FactHound offers a safe, fun way to find educator-approved Internet sites related to this book.

Here's what you do:

1. Visit *www.facthound.com*
2. Choose your grade level.
3. Begin your search.

This book's ID number is 9781429617246.

FactHound will fetch the best sites for you!

Index

Word Count: 139
Grade: 1
Early-Intervention Level: 18